Houghton
Mifflin
Harcourt

NATIONAL
JOURNEYS

Program Consultants
Shervaughnna Anderson · Marty Hougen
Carol Jago · Erik Palmer · Shane Templeton
Sheila Valencia · MaryEllen Vogt
Consulting Author · Irene Fountas

Unit 4

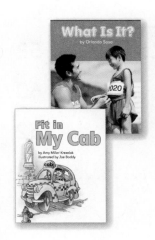

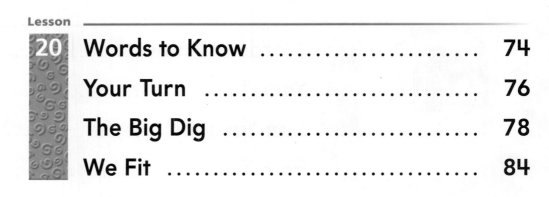

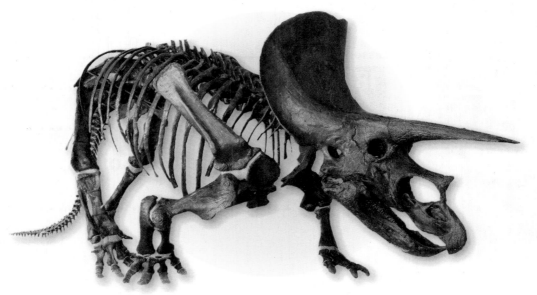

Unit 5

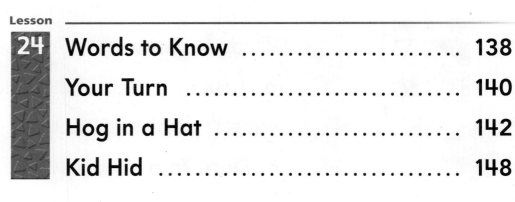

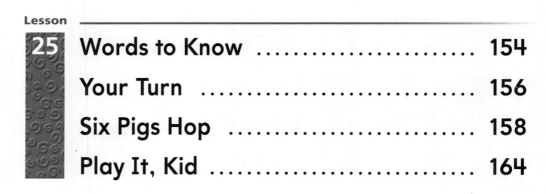
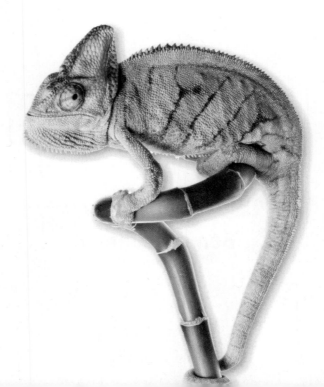

6

Unit 6

On Our Way

What Is It?
by Orlando Sosa

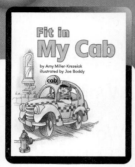
Fit in My Cab
by Amy Miller-Krezelak
illustrated by Joe Boddy

WORDS TO KNOW
High-Frequency Words

is
how
of
so
many
where

Vocabulary Reader

Camping Under the Stars

Context Cards

Words to Know

▶ Read the words.

▶ Talk about the pictures.

is

1

This **is** a planet.

how

2

This is **how** we see a planet.

10

of

3

Earth is the name **of** our planet.

so

4

This spaceship is **so** big!

many

5

See how **many** stars there are!

where

6

Where on Earth do you live?

Choose one word.
Use it in a sentence.

Your Turn

Talk About It!

What did you learn about science from the **Big Book?** Tell a partner.

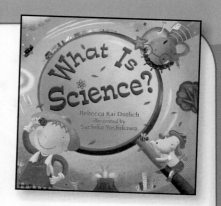

Write About It!

Draw and write about what you would like to study.

I love volcanoes.

Cameron

13

What Is It?

by Orlando Sosa

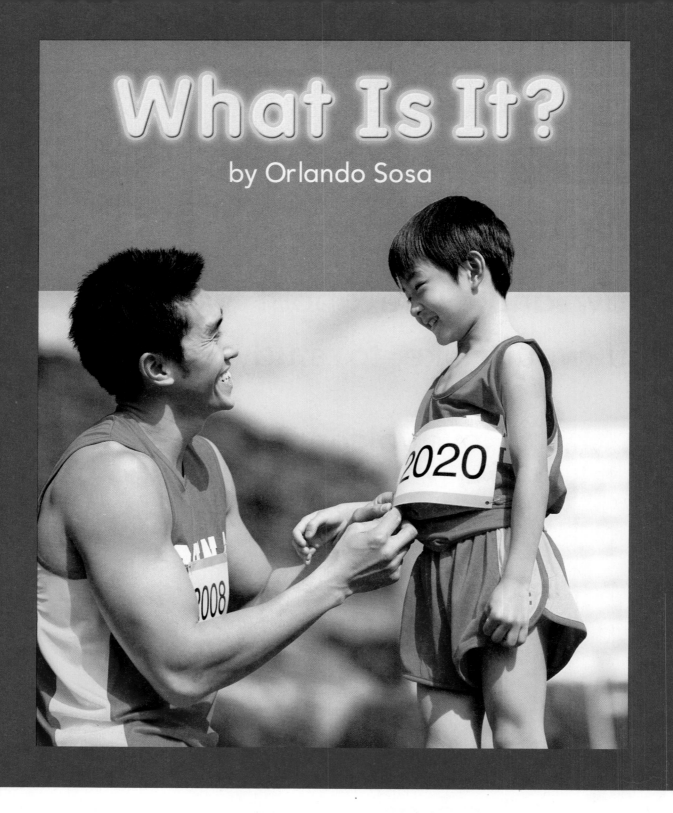

Tam can pin it.
See Tam pin it?
What can Tam pin?

Pat bit it.
Pat bit it and bit it.
What is it?

Sam can nip it. Nip, nip, nip.
What can Sam nip?

It can fit Cam.
What can fit Cam?
What is it?

Tim can pat it.
Tim can pat it and pat it.
What can Tim pat?

Where is Pam?
What can Pam see?
How can Pam see it?

Fit in My Cab

by Amy Miller-Krezelak
illustrated by Joe Boddy

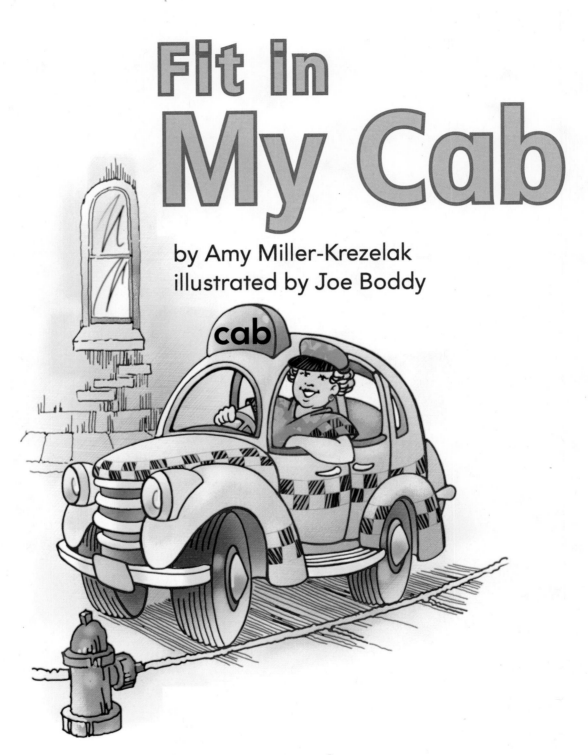

It is my cab.
I can fit in it.

Nat can sit in it.
Can Sam fit in it?

Sam can fit. Can Mac fit?
Mac can fit. Sit, Mac, sit!

How can Bab fit in it?
Bab can fit. Sit, Bab, sit!

Nat, Sam, Bab, and Mac can fit.
So, where can I fit in it?

Many can fit in my cab.

It is a bit of a fit in my cab.

WORDS TO KNOW

High-Frequency Words

this
find
from
came
but
on

Vocabulary
Reader

Context
Cards

Words to Know

▶ Read the words.

▶ Talk about the pictures.

this

Look at this big bug!

find

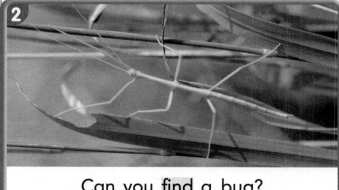

Can you find a bug?

from

The bee flew from flower to flower.

came

The butterfly came out of its chrysalis.

but

It doesn't look like it, but this will be a beautiful butterfly.

on

Do you see spots on the ladybug?

Choose one word.
Use it in a sentence.

Your Turn

Talk About It!

Talk about how the caterpillar in the **Big Book** changes. How do other living things change as they grow? Discuss with a partner.

Write About It!

Draw how a caterpillar becomes a butterfly. Label each stage.

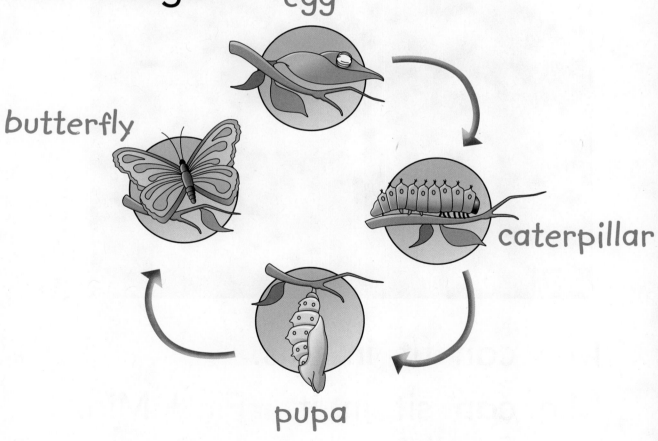

egg

butterfly

caterpillar

pupa

Can You Find It?

by Randi Livingston

Min can fit in this.

Min can sit in it. Find Min.

Tim can fit in this.
Tim can sit in it. Find Tim.

Pat can sit in this.
Pat can fit in it.

Sam can sit in the cap.
But the cap is big on Sam.

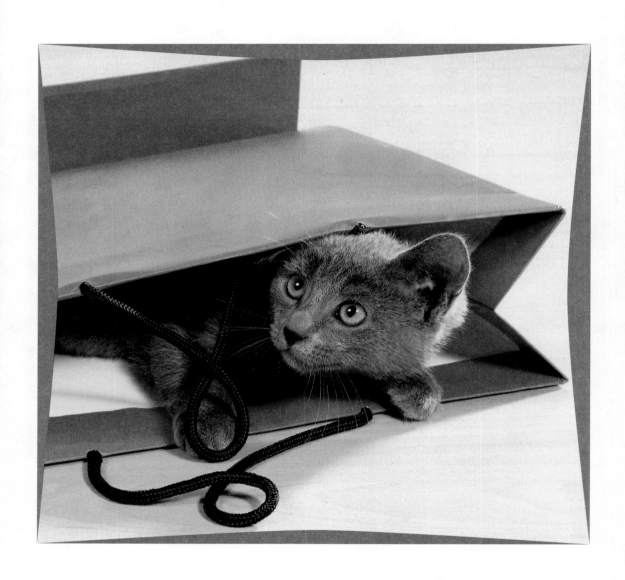

Tig can see me from this bag.
Tig can fit in it.

Nan can find Cam.
Tag! Now Cam is It!

Pam Pig

by Zev Herschel
illustrated by Liz Callen

This big pig is Pam Pig.
Can Pam Pig find Pat Cat?

This big cat is Pat Cat.
Can Pat Cat find Pam Pig?

Pam Pig sat.

Pam Pig came to find Pat Cat.

Can Pam Pig find Pat Cat?

Pat Cat sat.

Pat Cat came to find Pam Pig.

Can Pat Cat find Pam Pig?

Pam Pig can see Pat Cat.
Pat Cat can see Pam Pig.

Pat Cat can sit with Pam Pig.
Pam Pig and Pat Cat sat and sat.

Nat, Tim, and Tan Sam
by Daniel Osterman

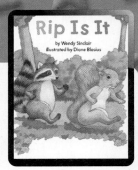
Rip Is It
by Wendy Sinclair
Illustrated by Diane Blasius

WORDS TO KNOW
High-Frequency Words

will
be
into
that
your
who

Vocabulary Reader

At the Beach
by Jake Volpe

Context Cards

Words to Know

▸ Read the words.

▸ Talk about the pictures.

will

We will look for a shark.

be

Fish can be great pets.

into

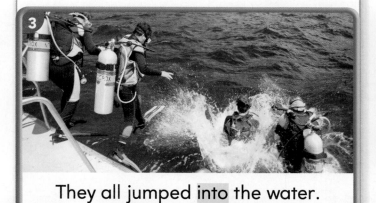

They all jumped into the water.

that

Can you see that whale?

your

Is your house near the ocean?

who

This is the man who fed the shark.

Choose one word.
Use it in a sentence.

Your Turn

Talk About It!

In what ways is the Atlantic Ocean important? Talk to a partner about it.

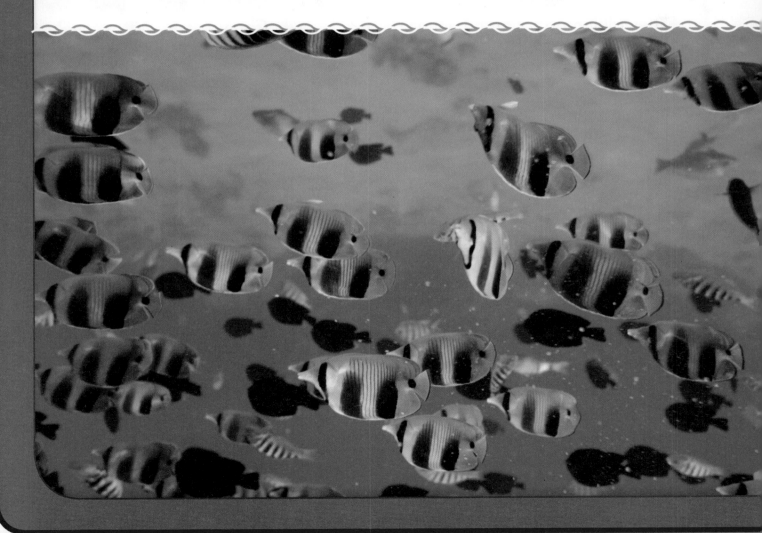

44

Write About It!

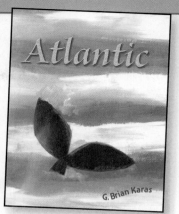

Atlantic

G. Brian Karas

Why is it important to care for oceans? Draw and write about it.

Fish need clean water.

Nat, Tim, and Tan Sam

by Daniel Osterman

I am Nat Cat.
Am I big?

Who is that big, big cat?
It is Nat Cat. Nat Cat is big.
Big Nat Cat can sit like your
big cat.

I am Tim Pig.
Am I big?

Who is that big, big pig?
It is Tim Pig. Tim Pig is big.
Big Tim can sip it and sip it.

I am Tan Sam.
Am I big?

It is Tan Sam! Tan Sam is big.
Big Tan Sam ran, ran, and sat.
Big Tan Sam can sit.

Rip Is It

by Wendy Sinclair
illustrated by Diane Blasius

Rip is It.   Rip ran.
Pam ran and ran.

Rip ran into Pam!
Rip can tag Pam.

Pam will be It now.
Can Pam tag Rip?

Rip is It.
Can Rip tag Pam?

Pam ran and ran.

Can Rip tag Pam now?

Go for It!
by William Alfred
illustrated by Jill Dubin

D Is for Dad
by David McCoy
illustrated by Lisa Thiesing

WORDS TO KNOW

High-Frequency Words

go

for

here

they

soon

up

Vocabulary Reader

Context Cards

Going for a Hike
by Minnie Ruhm
illustrated by
Bob Masheris
HOUGHTON MIFFLIN

Words to Know

Read Together

▶ Read the words.

▶ Talk about the pictures.

go

We go on a hike.

for

This backpack is for you.

here

We like to hike here in the hills.

they

They crossed the bridge.

soon

She will climb to the top soon.

up

They raced up the mountain.

Choose one word.
Use it in a sentence.

Your Turn

Talk About It!

What can happen on a hike?
Talk to a partner about it.
Use the **Big Book** for ideas.

Write About It!

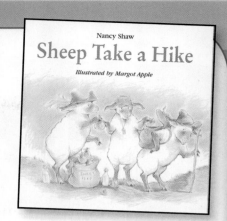

Sheep Take a Hike

What part of the story do you like best? Why? Draw and write about it.

I like it when they find the path.

Go for It!

by William Alfred
illustrated by Jill Dubin

Here is Pat. Pat can dig it.
Go for it, Pat!
Dig it, Pat. Dig it.

Nan can sit and dab it.
Go for it, Nan!
Dab it, Nan. Dab it.

Mim can sip it.
Go for it, Mim!
Sip it, Mim. Sip it.

Dan can tap it for sap.
Go for it, Dan!
Tap it, Dan. Tap it.

Sid can pat the big pig.
Go for it, Sid!
Pat the pig, Sid.

Tad and Pam can dip.
They go for it!
Dip, Tad!   Dip, Pam!

D Is for Dad

by David McCoy

illustrated by Lisa Thiesing

D is for Dad.
Dad, dad. Dad Pig is big.

Dad Pig can dig.
Dad Pig can dig it up.

Dad Pig can sit in a rig.
Dad Pig can dig in a rig.

Dad Pig is at bat.
Bat it, Dad! Bat it!
Soon I can be at bat.

Dad Pig can go in for a dip.
Dad Pig can go in big!

Dad, dad, my big Dad Pig.
I can be with big Dad Pig.

The Big Dig
by David Michaels
illustrated by Robin Koontz

We Fit
by Cindy Evans
illustrated by Tim Bowers

WORDS TO KNOW

High-Frequency Words

is
how
this
will
go
here

**Vocabulary
Reader**

**Context
Cards**

This is a planet.

Words to Know

Read
Together

▶ You learned these words.

is

This **is** a planet.

how

This is **how** we see a planet.

this

Look at this big bug!

will

We will look for a shark.

go

We go on a hike.

here

We like to hike here in the hills.

Now use each word in a sentence.

Your Turn

Read Together

Talk About It!

How do scientists study dinosaurs? Talk to a friend about it.

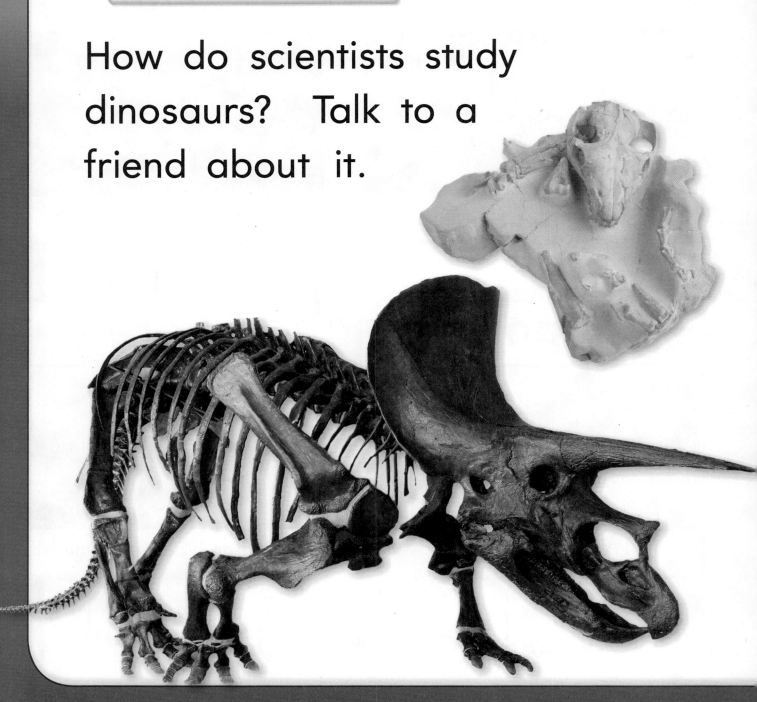

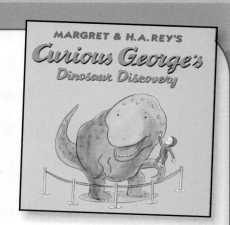

Write About It!

How does Curious George find dinosaur bones? Draw and write about it.

He digs.

He dusts.

The Big Dig

by David Michaels

illustrated by Robin Koontz

Pip will dig and dig.
Pip will go find Sid.

Tap, tap. Sid, are you here?
Tap, tap. Come and dig, Sid!

Sid is in.
Pip did find Sid.

Pip can dig.
Sid can dig with Pip.
Pip and Sid dig and dig.

Tim can dig with Pip.
Tim can dig with Sid.
Tim, Pip, and Sid can dig.

Pip can pat it.
Sid can pat it.
Tim can pat it.
It is big!

We Fit

by Cindy Evans

illustrated by Tim Bowers

Pit, pat, pit, pat, pit, pat.

Pit, pat, pit, pat, pit, pat.
Sid can sit here.
Sid can fit.

Pit, pat, pit, pat, pit.
Can Sam fit here?
Can Sam sit with Sid?

Pit, pat, pit, pat, pit.
Can Rib fit here?
Will Rib, Sam, and Sid sit?

Pit, pat, pit, pat, pit.
Sid can fit. Sam can fit.
Rib can fit.
How will Tim fit?

This is how Tim can fit.

Tim, Sam, Rib, and Sid sit.

Pit, pat, pit, pat, pit.

Make It Pop!
by Kari Matheson

My Dog, Tom
by Amy Miller-Krezelak
illustrated by Amanda Harvey

WORDS TO KNOW
High-Frequency Words

make
play
them
give
say
new

Vocabulary Reader

Friends
by Olivia Rose

HOUGHTON MIFFLIN

Context Cards

Words to Know

Read
Together

▸ Read the words.

▸ Talk about the pictures.

make

We **make** a tower.

play

We **play** baseball.

them

I like to hear **them** play music.

give

Music teachers **give** lessons.

say

We **say** the pledge to the flag.

new

I learned a **new** song.

Choose one word.
Use it in a sentence.

Your Turn

Talk About It!

How do musicians work together to make music? Talk about it with a partner.

Write About It!

Draw and write about your favorite instrument or musician in the **Big Book.**

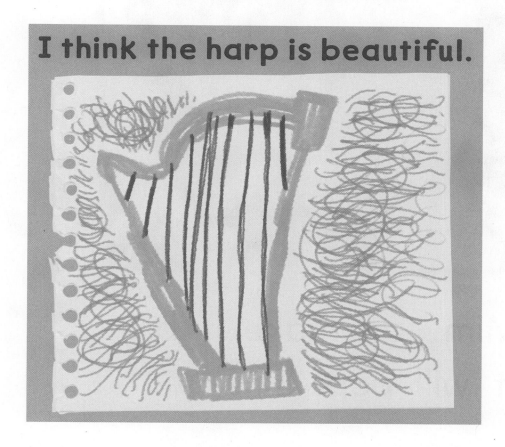

I think the harp is beautiful.

Make It Pop!

by Kari Matheson

Mim can make it big.
It will pop.

Tom can make it big.
Pop it, Tom! Pop it!

Dot and Pat play with them.
Pop it, Dot!
Pop it, Pat!

Cam can make it pop.
Pop it, Cam!
Pop it! Pop it!

Pam can make it pop!

Pop it, Pam!

Pop it!   Pop it!

Rob can make it big.
Will it pop, Rob?
I say it will! Pop it!

My Dog, Tom

by Amy Miller-Krezelak

illustrated by Amanda Harvey

Tom is my new dog.
Tom can sit with me.
I can pat Tom.

Tom can nap on this pad.
The pad is tan.
Nap on your pad, Tom.

Tom can nip it.

Give it, Tom!

Can Tom dig a pit?

Tom can dig a big pit.
Tom can dig and dig!
Can Tom play tag?

Tom can play tag.
I can tag Tom.
Tom can tag me.

Tom got big!
Tom and I got big.

A Good Job by Spiro Dantous

Fix It! by Sue Chang illustrated by John Berg

WORDS TO KNOW
High-Frequency Words

said

good

was

then

ate

could

Vocabulary Reader

Family Fun

Context Cards

Words to Know

▸ Read the words.

▸ Talk about the pictures.

said

My dad **said** I could ride my bike.

good

This watermelon tastes **good**!

was

It was our turn to do the dishes.

then

The baby played and then clapped her hands.

ate

Yesterday we ate lunch outside.

could

Did you know I could jump so high?

Choose one word.

Use it in a sentence.

Your Turn

Talk About It!

Think about the **Big Book**. How does Leo change as he grows up? Talk to a friend about it.

Leo the Late Bloomer
BY ROBERT KRAUS · PICTURES BY JOSE ARUEGO

Write About It!

Draw and write about a time you learned to do something new.

I can draw the sun.

A Good Job

by Spiro Dantous

Rod got a job in a rig.
Rod can sit in the rig.

"I got a job," said Jon.
Jon can dig.
Jon can give it a tap. Tap it, Jon!

Dom got a job in a cab.
Dom can sit in the cab.

Dot got a job. Dot can tap it.
Dot can fix it.
Tap it, Dot! Fix it!

Pam got a job.
Pam could mix jam. Mix it, Pam!
"Then I ate it," said Pam.

Max Dog got a good job.
Jan can not see. Max can.

Fix It!

by Sue Chang
illustrated by John Berg

The map got a rip in it.
"It was Ox," said Fox.
"Ox did it."

"It is a job for Ox!" said Dog.
"Fix it, Ox.
Fix the rip in the map."

Then the cap got a rip in it.
"Fox!" said Ox. "Fox did it."

"Fox can fix it," said Dog.
"Fox can sit and fix the cap."

The box got a big rip in it.
"I did it. I did it," said Dog.
"I can fix it, Ox."

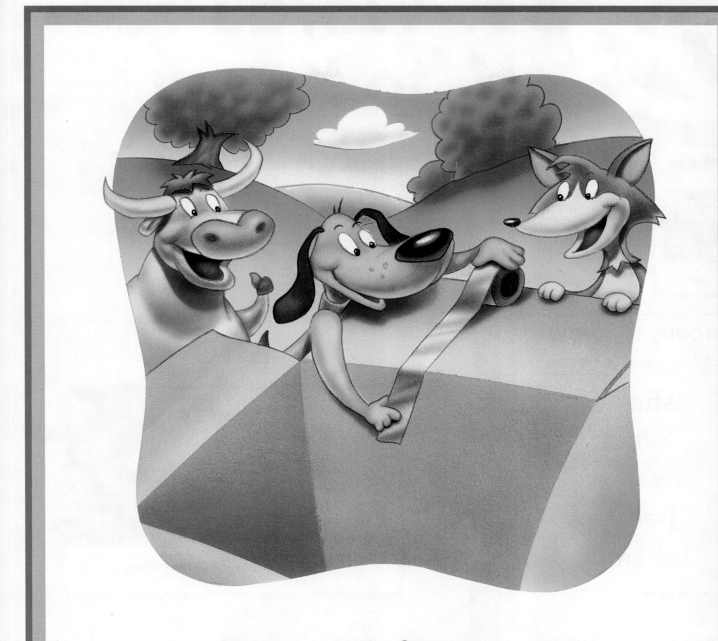

Dog did fix it.
Good job, Dog!

Lesson 23

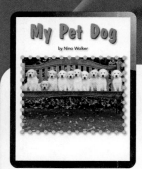

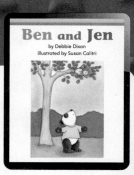

WORDS TO KNOW
High-Frequency Words

she
all
over
her
when
some

Vocabulary Reader

Context Cards

Words to Know

Read Together

▶ Read the words.

▶ Talk about the pictures.

she

She works in the garden.

all

Look at all the colorful flowers!

over

Will the puppy tip over the pot?

her

She wore her hat and gloves.

when

They planted the flowers when it was sunny.

some

Please give the plants some water.

Choose one word.
Use it in a sentence.

Your Turn

Talk About It!

What steps can someone follow to plant and grow flowers? Talk to a friend about it.

Zinnia's Flower Garden
·MONICA WELLINGTON·

Write About It!

Draw and write about flowers you would like to grow.

I want to grow a tulip.

My Pet Dog

by Nina Walker

All ten pets can sit.
All ten pets can fit
when they sit.

Ben is her pet dog.
Can Ben get a big pat?

Ted is her pet dog.
Can Ted get a big pat?

Deb ran, ran, ran.
What did she get?

Meg ran over here.
What did she get?

Peg can fit in the bag.
Peg can sit in it.

Ben and Jen

by Debbie Dixon
illustrated by Susan Calitri

"Jen, Jen, Jen!" said Ben.
"I can not get Jen."

"Get a net," said Ed.
Ben can not get Jen.

"Get a box," said Ted.
Ben can not get Jen.

Can Meg get Jen?
She can not get Jen.

Ed and Ted got some men.
Ben and Meg got some men.

"I can get Jen," said Meg.
Meg did it!
Meg did get Jen.

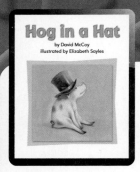

Hog in a Hat
by David McCoy
illustrated by Elizabeth Sayles

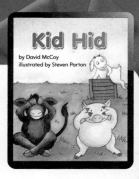

Kid Hid
by David McCoy
illustrated by Steven Parton

WORDS TO KNOW
High-Frequency Words

he

no

away

must

by

there

Vocabulary Reader

Context Cards

Words to Know

▸ Read the words.

▸ Talk about the pictures.

he

1

The chameleon is hungry when he wakes up.

no

2

There is no chameleon in this tree.

away

The zebras ran **away** from a lion.

must

This animal **must** hide in the snow.

by

The cheetahs wait side **by** side in the grass.

there

Do you see a fish hiding **there**?

Choose one word.
Use it in a sentence.

Your Turn

Read Together

Talk About It!

The **Big Book** tells how a chameleon can change colors. How do its colors help it survive? Talk about it with a friend.

Write About It!

Draw and write to share one interesting fact you learned about chameleons.

Hog in a Hat

by David McCoy

illustrated by Elizabeth Sayles

Hog can sit.

He can sit in a big top hat.

Dog can sit.
She can sit in a big red hat.

Cat can sit.

He can sit in a big tan hat.

Hen ran by.
She ran away in a red hat.

Fox can hop.

He can hop in a big hat.

Pig must nap now.
She can nap in a red hat.

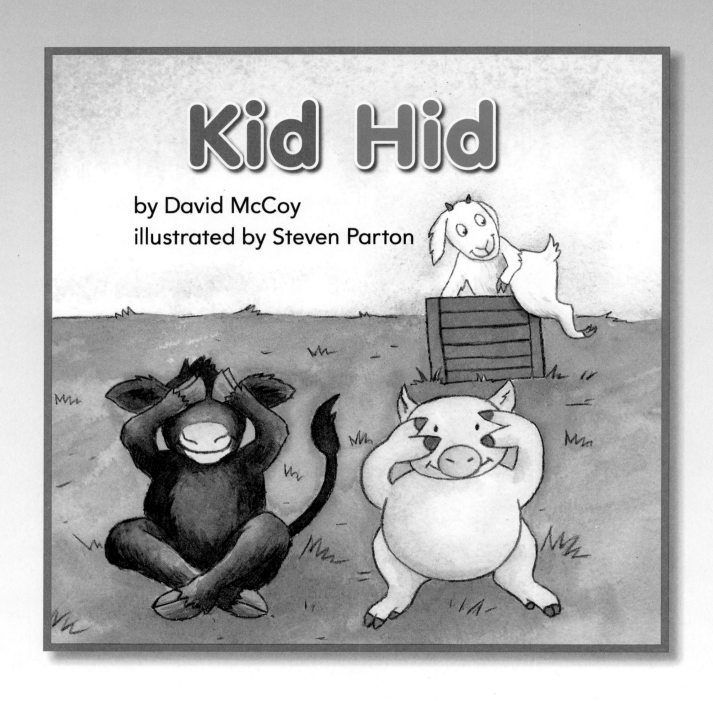

Kid Hid

by David McCoy

illustrated by Steven Parton

Kid hid.

Can he fit in the red box?

No, Kid can not fit in it.
Kim can find him in the box.

Kid hid in a bag.
The bag had a jet on it.
Can he fit in the bag?

No, Kid can not fit in there.
Ben can find him.

Can Kid fit in this big pot?
He hid in it.

Kim can not find him!
Ben can not find him!

Six Pigs Hop
by Diana Sheaffer
illustrated Kate Flanagan

Play It, Kid
by Franco Denehy
illustrated by Sarah Snow

WORDS TO KNOW
High-Frequency Words

play

over

good

said

all

she

Vocabulary Reader

Context Cards

Words to Know

Read Together

▶ You learned these words.

play

We play baseball.

over

Will the puppy tip over the pot?

good

This watermelon tastes good!

said

My dad said I could ride my bike.

all

Look at all the colorful flowers!

she

She works in the garden.

Now use each word in a sentence.

Your Turn

Talk About It!

How do people get food from plants? Share your ideas with a partner.

Write About It!

What kind of pie do you like best? Draw and write about it.

Six Pigs Hop

by Diana Sheaffer

illustrated Kate Flanagan

Six pigs sit in a pen.

"Sit, pigs," said Jen. "Be good."

Now, six pigs hop in the pen.
Hop, pigs! Jen is not here.

All six pigs hop and hop.

Hop, pigs. Hop.

Six pigs hop over the top.

Six pigs go for a dip.

Six pigs hop in.

Six pigs can play.

Six pigs can see Jen.
She can see six sad pigs.

Six pigs can sit.
Six pigs can dig in the pen.
Jen can see six pigs dig.

Play It, Kid

by Franco Denehy

illustrated by Sarah Snow

Dad Fox had a big box.
It had a tag on it.
Dad Fox hid the big box.

Red Hen ran by.
"It is a big box, said Red Hen.
"It has a tag."

The tag said Kid Fox.
"It is not for me," said Red Hen.
Red Hen hid the box.

Jon Dog can see the big box.
"It is for Kid Fox," said Jon Dog.

"It is not for me," said Jon Dog.
"Kid Fox! Kid Fox!
Here is a big box for Kid Fox."

Kid Fox got the big box.
It had a sax in it.
Kid Fox got the sax.
Play it, Kid!

Fun, Fun, Fun
by Bonnie Whitmark

Bug and Cat
by James Parsons
illustrated by John Hovell

WORDS TO KNOW
High-Frequency Words

down

do

went

only

little

just

Vocabulary Reader

I Can!
by Brady Hayes

Context Cards

Words to Know

▸ Read the words.

▸ Talk about the pictures.

down

We sit **down** to paint.

do

A dog can **do** lots of tricks.

went

This girl **went** swimming.

only

Only one kitten is out of the basket.

little

The **little** bunny is eating a carrot.

just

The girl **just** won the race.

Choose one word.
Use it in a sentence.

Your Turn

Talk About It!

In the **Big Book**, Kitten tries very hard to get a bowl of milk. Why is it important to try hard? Share your ideas with a partner.

172

Write About It!

What is your favorite part of the story? Draw and write about it.

Fun, Fun, Fun

Kit is in the bag.
Kit can fit in it.
Kit has fun in a bag.

What can little pups do for fun?
Pups can nip and tug.

Some pups just run.
It is fun to run.

Some dogs only dig for fun.
This big dog dug a lot.

Big dogs can run for fun.
It is fun to run in the sun.

This big cat ran up.
It went up and up.
Is it fun up there, Cat?

Bug and Cat

by James Parsons
illustrated by John Hovell

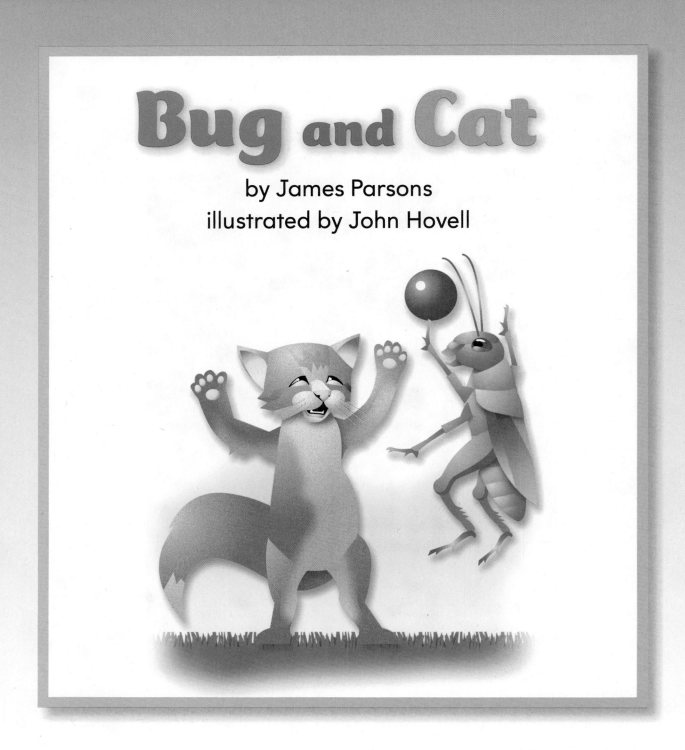

Bug and Cat can play.
Bug has it. Get it, Cat!
It is fun for Bug and Cat.

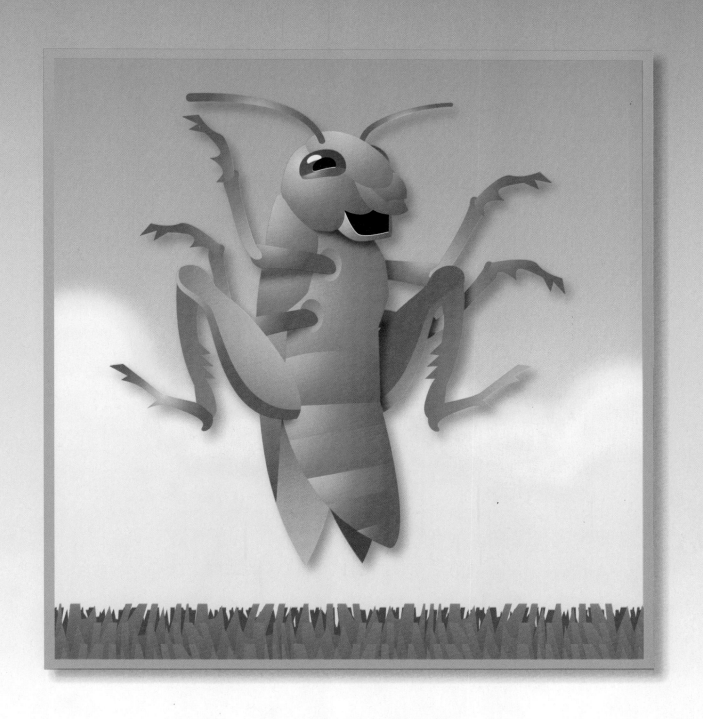

Bug can hop up and down.
Bug can hop with his six legs.

Cat can hit this for fun.
Rum, tum, tum!   Rum, tum!

Bug can hum. Cat can hum.
Hum, Bug. Hum, Cat.

Bug can sit on a rug.

Cat can sit on a rug.

It is fun for Bug and Cat.

Do Bug and Cat like to run?
Bug and Cat can run and run!
It is fun for Bug and Cat.

Win a Cup!
by Todd Turriro
illustrated by Marilyn Janovitz

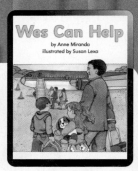

Wes Can Help
by Anne Miranda
illustrated by Susan Lexa

WORDS TO KNOW
High-Frequency Words

have
help
one
every
ask
walk

Vocabulary Reader

Let's Have Fun!
by Marty James

Context Cards

Words to Know

Read Together

▸ Read the words.

▸ Talk about the pictures.

have

I have one baby brother.

help

I help my mom draw.

one

This is the one I want.

every

We brush our teeth every morning.

ask

I ask for food when I am hungry.

walk

We walk in the park.

Choose one word.
Use it in a sentence.

Your Turn

Talk About It!

What is it like to be the youngest in a family? How does the youngest girl in the **Big Book** feel? Talk to a friend about it.

Write About It!

The girl in the story does many things. Draw and write about something she does that you would like to do.

Win a Cup!

by Todd Turriro

illustrated by Marilyn Janovitz

Meg can run and run!
Meg can win a big cup.

Ken can hit and run.
Ken can win a big cup.

Pam can hit every one down.
Pam can win a big cup.

Wes can help Lon.
Lon can help Wes win.

Wes can win a big cup!
Lon can win a big cup!

We all have a cup.

Wes Can Help

by Anne Miranda

illustrated by Susan Lexa

Len and Meg walk up to a big jet.
Len and Meg will have fun.

Wes led Len. Len can sit.
Wes led Meg. Meg can sit.

Len will ask Wes for help.
Wes got the big bag up.

Wes got Len a hot dog.
Wes got Meg a sub.

The big jet is down.
Len can run. Meg can run.

Len had fun. Meg had fun.
Wes had fun.

Vet on a Job!
by Anne Miranda

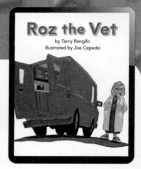
Roz the Vet
by Terry Rengifo
illustrated by Joe Cepeda

WORDS TO KNOW
High-Frequency Words

look

out

very

their

saw

put

Vocabulary Reader

Context Cards

Playing Ball

We look at the art.

Words to Know

▶ Read the words.

▶ Talk about the pictures.

look

We look at the art.

out

We camp out in the yard.

very

I play the piano **very** well.

their

They use **their** hands to play this game.

saw

The boy **saw** the toys.

put

She **put** the spoons away.

Choose one word.
Use it in a sentence.

Your Turn

Talk About It!

Why is it important to help your friends? Share your ideas with a partner.

Write About It!

Think about things that Curious George does in the **Big Book** story. Draw and write about something he does.

He **fl**ew a kite.

Vet on a Job!

by Anne Miranda

Pets like their vets.
Vets can help pets.

Dot is a vet.
Dot saw Bud.
Dot fed Bud. Sip it, Bud.

Val is a vet.
Val can look at Vin.
Vin can run now.

Zeb is very sad.
Zeb can not hop.
Bev the vet can look at Zeb.

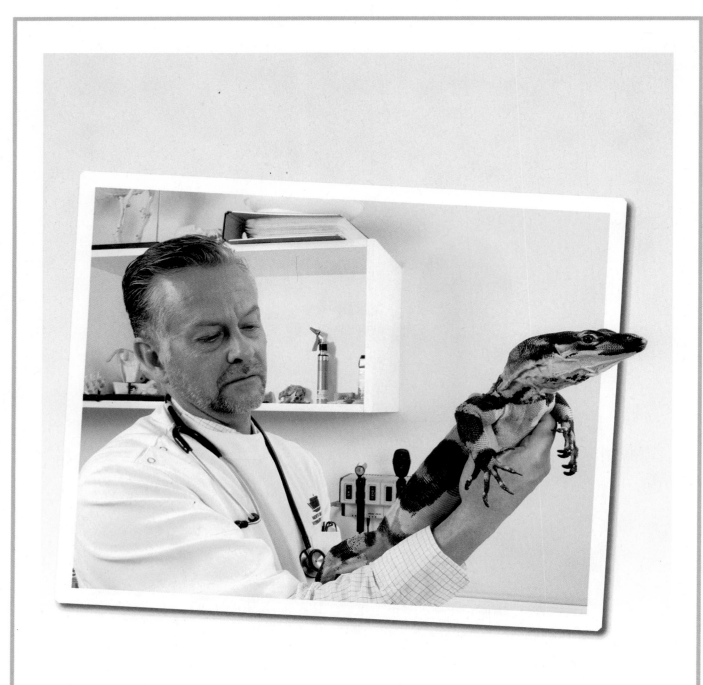

Vic is a vet.

Vic can look at Zip.

Zip can not get out.

Lil is a vet.

Lil can look at Sam.

Lil can pet Sam.

Roz the Vet

by Terry Rengifo

illustrated by Joe Cepeda

Roz the vet can help a pet!
Roz can zip in her red van.

Roz can look at a pet pig.
Roz fed the little pig.

Roz the vet can help a pet!
Roz can zip in her red van.

Vic had a bad cut.
Roz put Vic in the van.
Roz can fix it, Vic!

Tab Cat got out.

Tab ran up. Tab had fun.

Tab can not get down.

Tab saw Roz.
Roz can get Tab.

Not Yet
by Nancy Spencer

Can Not Quit Yet
by Antonio Winkler
illustrated by Rick Brown

WORDS TO KNOW
High-Frequency Words

off
take
our
day
too
show

Vocabulary Reader

Context Cards

Words to Know

Read Together

▸ Read the words.

▸ Talk about the pictures.

off

We get **off** the bus.

take

We **take** turns.

our

We raise our hands.

day

We show the weather for each day.

too

We draw houses.
We draw people, too.

show

We show our pictures.

Choose one word.
Use it in a sentence.

Your Turn

Talk About It!

What did you learn in kindergarten? Talk about it with a partner.

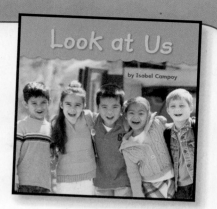

Look at Us

by Isabel Campoy

Write About It!

What can you do now that you couldn't do before kindergarten? Draw and write about it.

Not Yet

by Nancy Spencer

Cat, do not get up yet!
Nap on the little red mat.

Dog, do not get up yet!
Nap on the big rug all day.

Hen, do not get up yet!
Nap in the hen box.

Pig, do not get up yet!
Nap in the pig pen.

Fox, do not get up yet!
Nap in the fox den.

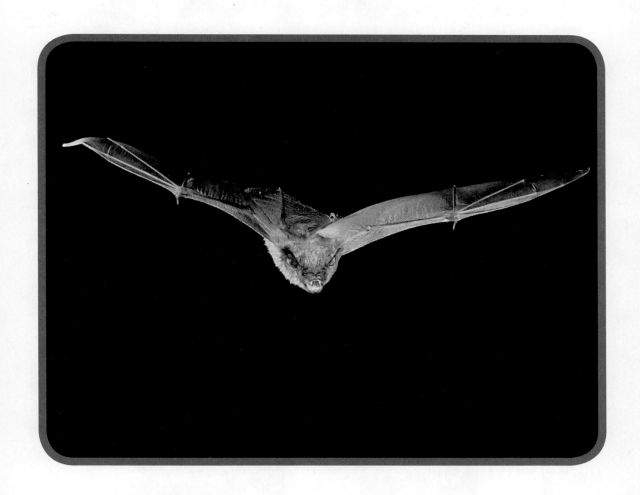

Bat, get up!   Bat, take off!
Bats only quit at sun up!

Can Not Quit Yet

by Antonio Winkler

illustrated by Rick Brown

Ben can hit it.

Jan and Rob play, too.

They can not quit yet.

Ben did not quit.
Show us how to do it, Ben.

Yes, yes! Tim can dig.
Tim can dig with Kim.

Kim can dig in the sun.
Kim will not quit yet.

Yes! Meg can zip the jet.
Our jets can take off.

Sal can zip the jet.
Meg will not quit yet.

Lesson
30

WORDS TO KNOW
High-Frequency Words

down

ask

help

walk

look

show

Vocabulary Reader

Context Cards

Words to Know

▶ You learned these words.

down

We sit **down** to paint.

ask

I **ask** for food when I am hungry.

help

I help my mom draw.

walk

We walk in the park.

look

We look at the art.

show

We show our pictures.

Now use each word in a sentence.

Your Turn

Talk About It!

What can you do to be a good friend? Share ideas with a partner.

Write About It!

Write about your favorite part of the story.

I like the pizza party.

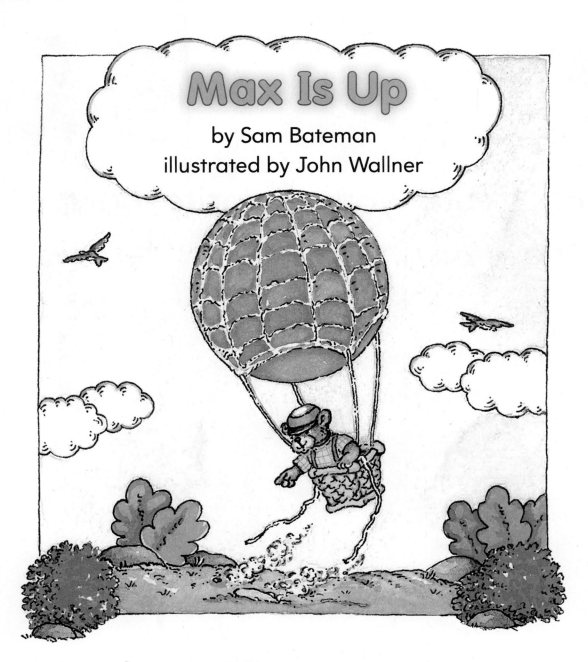

Max Is Up

by Sam Bateman

illustrated by John Wallner

Look at Max!
Max will go up, up, up.

Max is up.

Max can not get down.

"Help!" said Max.

Bud ran.

Can Bud get Max down?

Look! Bud can not get Max.

Tom ran to get Max.

Tom can not get him.

We can ask Big Ben to help us.

Big Ben can tug, tug, tug.
Will Max get down?
Tug, Big Ben, tug!
Will Max get down?

Yes. He did!
Big Ben got Max down.

A Fun Job

by Priscilla Banab

illustrated by Jeff Mack

Ted has a job.

Deb has a job.

"Find nuts," said Mom.
"Get nuts. Get lots of nuts."
Ted and Deb walk to get nuts.

Ted got nuts. Deb got nuts.
It is a fun job to get nuts.
Ted had fun. Deb had fun.

Ted can show Deb what to do.
Ted hid nuts in pots.
Deb hid nuts in pots.

Look at the pots.
Can Ted and Deb see nuts?
No, Ted and Deb can not.

Ted hid nuts in pots.
Deb hid nuts in pots.
What is in the pots now?

On Our Way

Long *i, o, e* Words

| so | me | I | We |

1. _____
   _____ am at bat.

2. _____
   _____ can play.

3. It is _____ hot!

4. Look at _____ !

How Can We Go?

by Kate Arnold   illustrated by Stephen Lewis

I am Tim. I can go.

Mom and Dad will go with me.

How can we go?

What will we see?

We can find a map.

It will help us.

We can go and go.

We will see a lot.

We can go in a van.
We will see a lot of big cats.
Will we see a cub? Yes!

We can go in a cab.
We will see a big fin.
Will we get wet? No!

We can go on a bus.
We will see a man at bat.
Will he get a hit?
Yes! Go! Go! Go!

We can go on a jet.
We will see a lot.
It will be so fun!

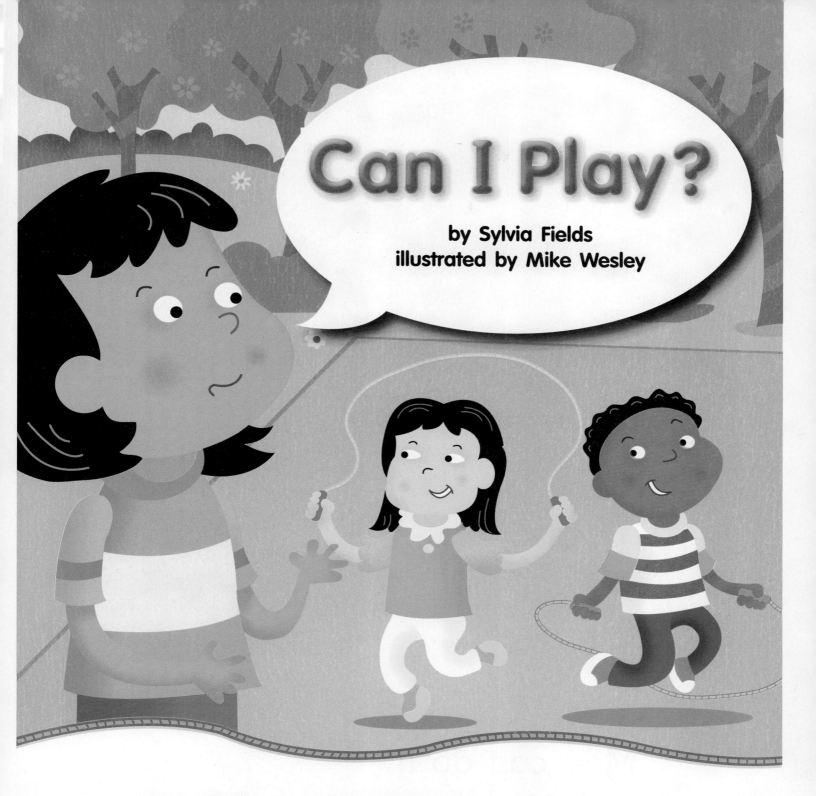

Can I Play?

by Sylvia Fields
illustrated by Mike Wesley

"Hi, Meg. Hi, Tim," said Jan.
"Can I do it? Can I play?"
"Yes, Jan. Yes!" they said.

259

Meg can do it.
Meg can go, go, go.
Go, Meg, go!

Tim can do it.

"Can you do it, Jan?" said Tim.

"No," said Jan. "I can not."

Meg and Tim can help Jan.
Meg and Tim can fix it.

"Look at me!" said Jan.
"I can do it!"
"Go, Jan, go!" said Meg and Tim.

"Hi, Ben!" said Jan.
"Come on!
We can all play."

tape

gate

cane

rake

game

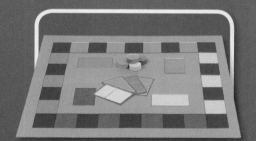

Long *i* Words

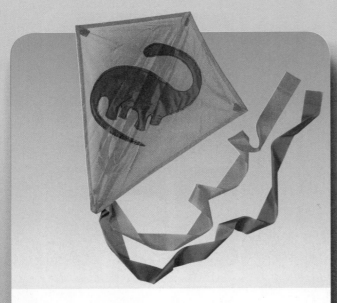

kite   kit

pine   pin

dim   dime

time   Tim

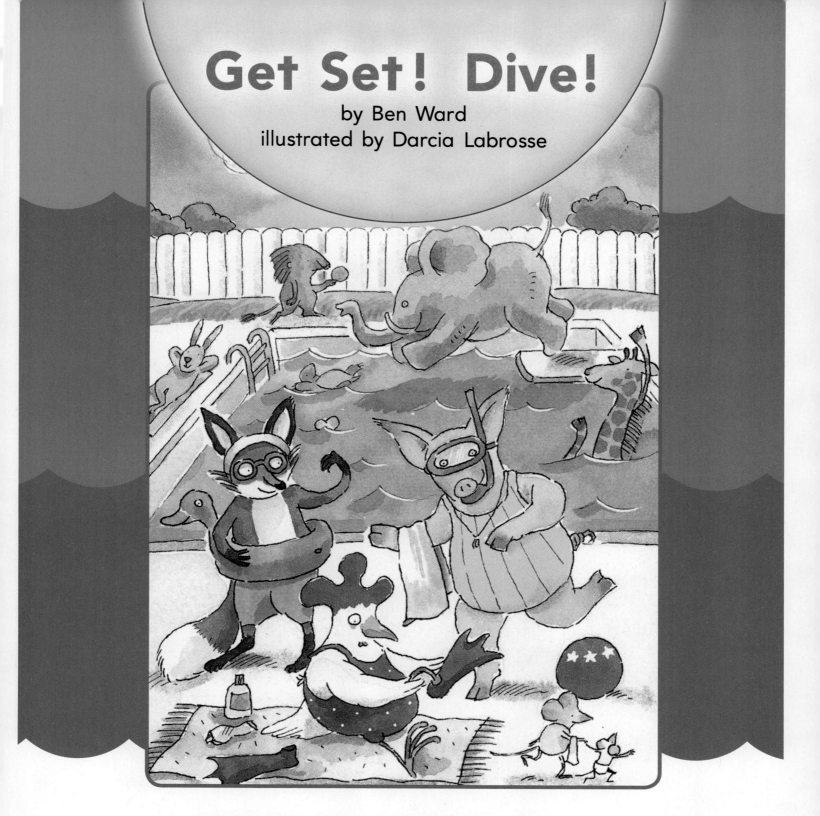

Get Set! Dive!

by Ben Ward

illustrated by Darcia Labrosse

"Come," said Fox.

"We can dive.

We can make a big wave."

Can Hen dive?

Get set! Dive! Hen can do it!

Hen can make a big wave.

Can Pig dive?

Get set! Dive! Pig can do it!

Pig can make a big wave.

Can Fox dive?

Get set! Dive! Fox can do it!

"This is fun," said Fox.

"Look!" said Pig.
"We can play a game.
We will get wet."

"Yes!" said Fox.
"It is time to play.
We will make a fine wave."
Look out!

Activity Central

Long *o* Words

1 tote tot

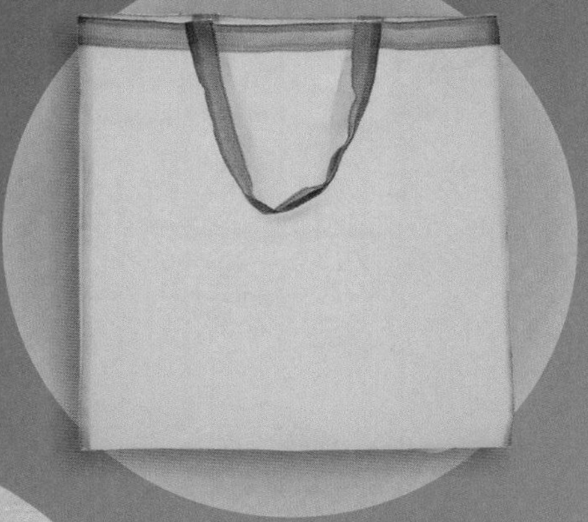

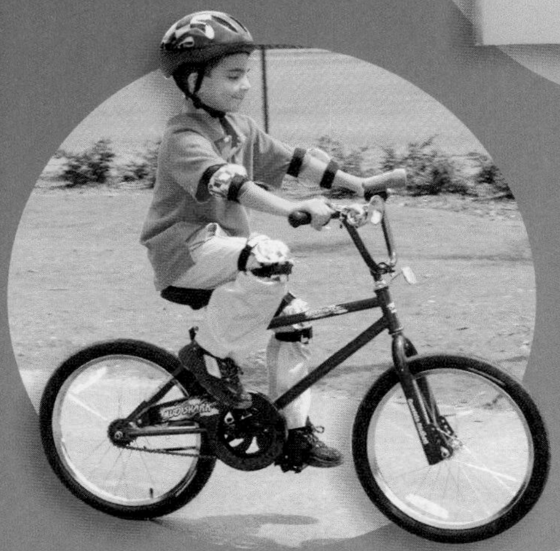

2 rod rode

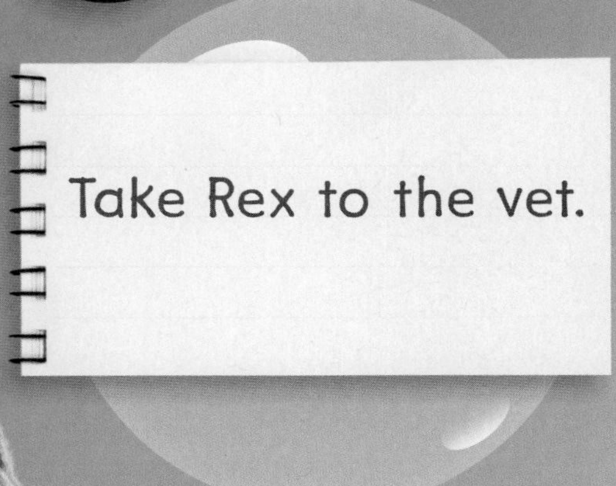
Take Rex to the vet.

3 not note

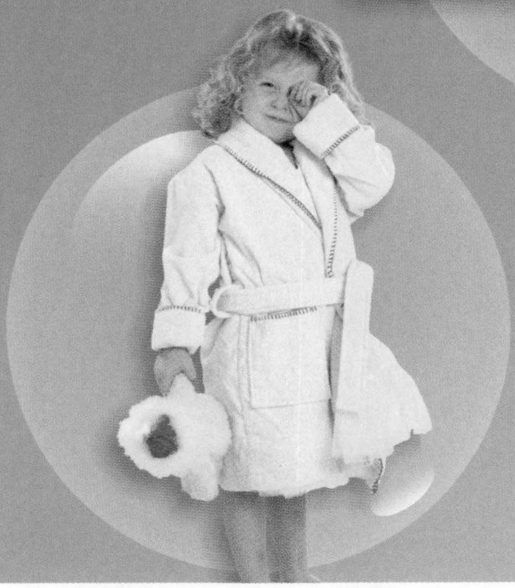

4 robe Rob

Long *u* Words

June   dune   tube   cubes

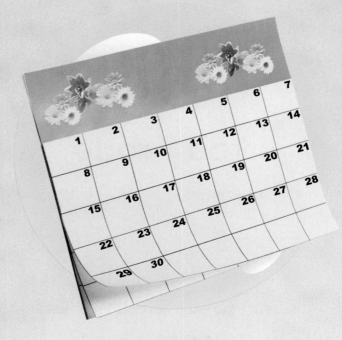

Luke, June, and Rose

by Denise Daniels

illustrated by Diane Palmisciano

Rose is in the mud!

Luke and June will not pat Rose.

Rose can get in the big tub.
June can use the hose.
"It will be fun, Rose!" said Luke.

"I am so wet," said Luke.
"Rose is not wet yet.
Get the hose in the tub, June."

Luke rubs Rose.

"Look, no mud!" said Luke.

Luke and June do a fine job.

"No, Rose! No!" said June.
"Do not get me wet!"

"Rose is so cute," said Mom.
"She is a good dog.
I will give Rose a big bone."

Word Lists

Unit 4

Lesson

16

What Is It?		Fit in My Cab	
Decodable Words	**High-Frequency Words**	**Decodable Words**	**High-Frequency Words**
Target Skill: Words with Short *i*	and, how, is, see, what, where	Target Skill: Words with Short *i*	a, and, how, I, is, many, my, of, so, where
bit, Cam, can*, fit, it*, nip, Pam, pat, pin, Sam, Tam, Tim		Bab, bit, cab, can*, fit, in*, it*, Mac, Nat, Sam, sit*	

Lesson

17

Can You Find It?		Pam Pig	
Decodable Words	**High-Frequency Words**	**Decodable Words**	**High-Frequency Words**
Target Skill: Words with *g*	but, find, from, is, me, now, on, see, the, this, you	Target Skill: Words with *g*	and, came, find, is, see, this, to, with
bag, big*, Cam, can*, cap, fit, in*, it*, Min, Nan, Pat, Sam, sit*, tag, Tig, Tim		big*, can*, cat, Pam, Pat, pig, sat, sit*	

Lesson

18

Nat, Tim, and Tan Sam		Rip Is It	
Decodable Words	**High-Frequency Words**	**Decodable Words**	**High-Frequency Words**
Target Skill: Words with *r*	and, I, is, like, that, who, your	Target Skill: Words with *r*	and, be, into, is, now, will
am*, big*, can*, cat, it*, Sam, Nat, pig, ran*, sip, sat, sit*, tan, Tim		can*, it*, Pam, ran*, Rip, tag	

Lesson

19

Go for It!		D Is for Dad	
Decodable Words	**High-Frequency Words**	**Decodable Words**	**High-Frequency Words**
Target Skill: Words with *d*	and, for, go, here, is, the, they	Target Skill: Words with *d*	a, be, for, go, I, is, my, soon, up, with
big*, can*, dab, Dan, dig, dip, it*, Mim, Nan, Pam, pat, pig, sap, Sid, sip, sit*, Tad, tap		at*, bat, big*, can*, dad, dig, dip, in*, it*, pig, rig, sit*	

Lesson 20

The Big Dig

Decodable Words

Review Short *i, g, r, d*

big*, can*, did*, dig, in*, it*, pat, Pip, Sid, tap, Tim

High-Frequency Words

and, are, come, find, go, here, is, the, will, with, you

We Fit

Decodable Words

Review Short *i, g, r, d*

can*, fit, pat, pit, Rib, Sam, Sid, sit*, Tim

High-Frequency Words

and, here, how, is, this, we, will, with

Unit 5

Lesson 21

Make It Pop!

Decodable Words

Target Skill: Words with Short *o*

big*, Cam, can*, Dot, it* Mim, Pam, Pat, pop, Rob, Tom

High-Frequency Words

and, I, make, play, say, them, will, with

My Dog, Tom

Decodable Words

Target Skill: Words with Short *o*

big*, can*, dig, dog, got*, is*, it*, nap, nip, on*, pad, pat, pit, sit*, tag, tan, Tom

High-Frequency Words

a, and, give, I, me, my, new, play, the, this, with, your

Lesson 22

A Good Job

Decodable Words

Target Skill: Words with *j, x*

cab, can*, dig, dog, Dom, Dot, fix, got*, in*, it*, jam, Jan, job, Jon, Max, mix, not*, Pam, rig, Rod, sit*, tap

High-Frequency Words

a, ate, could, give, good, I, said, see, the, then

Fix It!

Decodable Words

Target Skill: Words with *j, x*

big*, box, can*, cap, did*, dog, fix, fox, got*, in*, is*, it*, job, map, ox, rip, sit*

High-Frequency Words

and, a, for, good, I, said, the, then, was

Lesson 23

My Pet Dog

Decodable Words

Target Skill: Words with Short *e*

bag, Ben, big*, can*, Deb, did*, dog, fit, get*, in*, is*, it*, Meg, pat, Peg, pet, pets, ran*, sit*, Ted, ten

High-Frequency Words

a, all, her, here, my, over, she, the, they, what, when

Ben and Jen

Decodable Words

Target Skill: Words with Short *e*

Ben, box, can*, did*, Ed, get*, got*, it*, Jen, Meg, men, net, not*, Ted

High-Frequency Words

a, and, I, said, she, some

Lesson 24

Hog in a Hat

Decodable Words

Target Skill: Words with *h, k*

big*, can*, cat, dog, fox, hat, hen, hog, hop, in*, nap, pig, ran*, red, sit*, tan, top

High-Frequency Words

a, away, by, he, must, now, she

Kid Hid

Decodable Words

Target Skill: Words with *h, k*

Ben, bag, big*, box, can*, fit, had*, hid, him*, in*, it*, jet, Kid, Kim, not*, on*, pot, red

High-Frequency Words

a, find, he, no, the, there, this

Lesson 25

Six Pigs Hop

Decodable Words

Review Short *o*, Short *e, h, k, j, x*

can*, dig, dip, get*, hop, in*, is*, Jen, not*, pen, pigs, sit*, six, top, sad

High-Frequency Words

a, all, and, be, for, go, good, here, now, over, play, said, see, she, the

Play It, Kid

Decodable Words

Review Short *o*, Short *e, h, k, j, x*

big*, box, can*, dad, dog, fox, got*, had*, has*, hen, hid, in*, is*, it*, Jon, kid, not*, on*, ran*, red, sax, tag

High-Frequency Words

a, by, for, here, me, play, said, see, the

Unit 6

Lesson 26

Fun, Fun, Fun

Decodable Words

Target Skill: Words with Short *u*

bag, big*, can*, cat, dig, dog, dogs, dug, fit, fun, has*, in*, is*, it*, kit, lot, nip, pups, ran*, run*, sun, tug, up*

High-Frequency Words

a, and, do, for, just, little, only, some, the, there, this, to, went, what

Bug and Cat

Decodable Words

Target Skill: Words with Short *u*

bug, can*, cat, fun, get*, has*, his*, hit, hop, hum, is*, it*, legs, on*, rug, rum, run*, sit, six, tum, up*

High-Frequency Words

a, and, do, down, for, like, play, this, to, with

Lesson 27

Win a Cup!

Decodable Words

Target Skill: Words with *l, w*

big*, can*, cup, hit, Ken, Lon, Meg, Pam, run*, Wes, win

High-Frequency Words

a, all, and, down, every, have, help, one, we

Wes Can Help

Decodable Words

Target Skill: Words with *l, w*

bag, big*, can*, dog, fun, got*, had*, hot, is*, jet, led, Len, Meg, run*, sit*, sub, up*, Wes

High-Frequency Words

a, and, ask, down, for, have, help, the, to, walk, will

283

Lesson 28

Vet on a Job!

Decodable Words

Target Skill: Words with *v, z*

at*, Bev, bud, can*, dot, fed, get*, hop, is*, it*, job, Lil, not*, on*, pet, pets, run*, sad, Sam, sip, Val, vet, vets, Vic, Vin, Zeb, zip

High-Frequency Words

a, help, is, like, look, now, out, saw, the, their, very

Roz the Vet

Decodable Words

Target Skill: Words with *v, z*

at*, bad, can*, cat, cut, fed, fix, fun, get*, got*, had*, in*, it*, not*, pet, pig, ran*, red, Roz, sip, tab, up*, van, vet, Vic, zip

High-Frequency Words

a, down, help, her, little, look, out, put, saw, the

Lesson 29

Not Yet

Decodable Words

Target Skill: Words with *y, qu*

at*, bat, bats, big*, box, cat, den, dog, fox, get*, hen, in*, mat, nap, not*, on*, pen, pig, quit, red, rug, sun, up*, yet

High-Frequency Words

all, day, do, little, off, only, take, the

Can Not Quit Yet

Decodable Words

Target Skill: Words with *y, qu*

Ben, can*, did*, dig, hit, in*, it*, Jan, jet, jets, Kim, Meg, not*, quit, Rob, Sal, sun, Tim, us*, yes*, yet, zip

High-Frequency Words

and, do, how, off, our, play, show, take, the, they, to, too, will, with

Lesson 30

Max Is Up

Decodable Words

Short Vowel Review

at*, big*, Ben, bud, can*, did*, get*, got*, him*, is*, Max, not*, ran*, Tom, tug, up*, us*, yes*

High-Frequency Words

ask, down, go, he, help, look, said, to, we, will

A Fun Job

Decodable Words

Short Vowel Review

at*, can*, Deb, fun, get*, got*, had*, has*, hid, in*, is*, it*, job, lots, Mom, not*, nuts, pots, Ted

High-Frequency Words

a, and, do, find, look, no, of, said, see, show, the, to, now, walk, what

How Can We Go?

Decodable Words

Target Skill: Words with Long *e, i, o* (CV)

am*, at*, bat, be*, big*, bus, cab, can*, cats, cub, dad, fin, fun, get*, go*, he*, hit, I*, in*, it*, jet, lot, man*, map, me*, mom, no*, on*, so*, Tim, us*, van, we*, wet, yes*

High-Frequency Words

a, and, find, help, how, of, see, what, will, with

Can I Play?

Decodable Words

Target Skill: Words with Long *e, i, o* (CV)

at*, Ben, can*, fix, go*, hi, I*, it*, Jan, me*, Meg, no*, not*, on*, Tim, we*, yes*

High-Frequency Words

all, and, come, do, help, look, play, said, they, you

Get Set! Dive!

Decodable Words

Target Skill: Words with Long *a, i* (CVCe)

big*, can*, dive, fine, fox, fun, game, get*, hen, is*, it*, make*, pig, set, time*, wave, we*, wet, yes*

High-Frequency Words

a, come, do, look, out, play, said, this, to, will

Luke, June, and Rose

Decodable Words

Target Skill: Words with Long *o, u* (CVCe)

am*, be*, big*, bone, can*, cute, dog, fine, fun, get*, hose, I*, in*, is*, it*, job, June, Luke, me*, mom, mud, no*, not*, pat, Rose, rubs, so*, tub, use*, wet, yet

High-Frequency Words

a, and, do, give, good, look, said, she, the, will

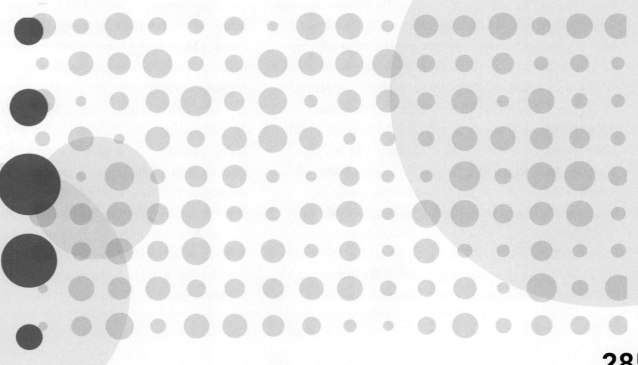

Photo Credits

Placement Key: (r) right, (l) left, (c) center, (t) top, (b) bottom, (bg) background

3 (tl) Gareth Brown/Corbis; (cl) Juniors Bildarchiv/Alamy; (bl) Pick and Mix Images/Alamy; **4** (b) ©Alamy Images; **5** (tl) Digital Vision/Getty Images; (tl) Owaki – Kulla/Corbis; (cl) M Stock/Alamy; (bl) Photofusion Picture Library/Alamy; **6** (tl) ©Getty Images (b) ©Maria Gritsai/Alamy; **7** (tl) Comstock/Jupiter Images; (b) Getty Images; **8** (tl) © Corbis; (cl) Gary Dyson/Alamy; **9** (tl) ©Marzanna Syncerz/Fotolia; (b) Jupiter Unlimited; **10** (tl) Gareth Brown/Corbis; (t) ©StockTrek/Corbis; (b) Charles C Place/Photographer's Choice RF/Getty Images; **11** (tl) Digital Vision/Getty Images; (tr) Getty Images/Photodisc; (bl) ©Photick/Alamy; (br) Houghton Mifflin Harcourt; **12** Houghton Mifflin Harcourt; **14** Gareth Brown/Corbis; **15** Turbo/zefa/Corbis; **16** moodboard/Corbis; **17** Roy Morsch/Corbis; **18** © Paul Barton/Corbis; **19** Burke/Triolo Productions/Brand X/Corbis; **26** (tl, t) Juniors Bildarchiv/Alamy; (b) Ted Kinsman/Photo Researchers, Inc.; **27** (tl) © Paul Melling/Alamy; (tr) ©Creatas/Getty Images; (bl) ©Digital Vision/Getty Images; (br) ©Radius Images/Getty Images; **28** © Roy McMahon/Corbis; **30** Juniors Bildarchiv/Alamy; **31** Design Pics Inc./Alamy; **32** Digital Vision/Alamy; **33** Eye Candy Images/Alamy; **34** © Woodfall Wild Images/Alamy; **35** © Dave Porter/Alamy; **42** (tl) Pick and Mix Images/Alamy; (t) Porky Pies Photography/Alamy; (b) Barbara Maurer/Stone/Getty Images; **43** (tl) Image Source /Getty Images; **44** Photodisc/Getty Images; **46** Pick and Mix Images/Alamy; **47** © Hugh Threlfall/Alamy; **48** © Juniors Bildarchiv/Alamy; **49** © Juniors Bildarchiv/Alamy; **50** © Neil Hardwick/Alamy; **51** © Penny Boyd/Alamy; **58** (t) ©LOOK Die Bildagentur der Fotografen GmbH/Alamy Images; (b) Tom Grill/Corbis; **59** (tl) Jupiterimages/Getty Images; (tr) ©moodboard/Corbis; (bl) Jupiterimages/Getty Images; (br) ©Juice Images/Alamy; **60** Houghton Mifflin Harcourt; (tr) © Westend **61**/Alamy; (bl) Goodshoot/Jupiterimages/Getty Images; (br) © Corbis; **74** (t) ©StockTrek/Corbis; (b) Charles C Place/Photographer's Choice RF/Getty Images; **75** (tl) Juniors Bildarchiv/Alamy; (tr) Porky Pies Photography/Alamy; (bl) ©LOOK Die Bildagentur der Fotografen GmbH/Alamy Images; (br) ©moodboard/

Corbis; **76** (t) ©Jupiterimages/Getty Images; (b) ©Alamy Images; **90** (tl) © Owaki – Kulla/Corbis; (t) Jose Luis Pelaez/Iconica/Getty Images; (b) Image Source/Superstock; **91** (tl) Houghton Mifflin Harcourt; (tr) Adobe Image Library/Getty Images; (bl) Bananastock/Jupiterimages/Getty Images; (br) Somos Images/Alamy; **92** (tr) ©Houghton Mifflin Harcourt; (bl) Creatas/Getty Images; (c) Creatas/Getty Images; (br) Creatas/Getty Images; **94** Owaki – Kulla/Corbis; **95** © Itani/Alamy; **96** © Butch Martin/Alamy; **97** © Inspirestock Inc./Alamy; **98** © Imagehit Inc./Alamy; **99** © Rubberball/Alamy; **106** (tl) Owaki – Kulla/Corbis; (t) Fransisco Cruz/Superstock; (b) Rubberball/Superstock; **107** (tl, tr) Brand X Pictures\Getty Images; (bl and br) Houghton Mifflin Harcourt; **108** Houghton Mifflin Harcourt; **110** M Stock/Alamy; **111** ©Stefanie Grewel/Getty Images; **112** © Jupiterimages/Brand X/Alamy; **113** © Blend Images/Alamy; **114** © pixland/Corbis; **115** © Photofusion Picture Library/Alamy; **122** (tl) Photofusion Picture Library/Alamy; (t) Chip Henderson/Index Stock Imagary/Jupiterimages; (b) Ross Pictures/Botanica/Jupiterimages; **123** (tl) BananaStock/Jupiterimages/Getty Images; (tr, bl, br) Houghton Mifflin Harcourt; **124** Houghton Mifflin Harcourt; **126** Photofusion Picture Library/Alamy; **127** © Corbis Premium RF/Alamy; **128** Brian Sytnyk/Masterfile; **129** © AM Corporation/Alamy; **130** © tbkmedia.de/Alamy; **131** © Jim Zuckerman/Alamy; **138** (t) Nigel J. Dennis/Gallo Images/Getty Images; (b) Peter Adams Photography/Alamy; **139** (tl) Corbis; (tr) ©Stephen Lackie/Corbis; (bl) Brand X Pictures/Getty Images; (br) ©Sandy Jones/Getty Images; **140** Renaud Visage/Photographer's Choice RF/Getty Images; **141** ©Maria Gritsai/Alamy; **154** (t) Image Source/Superstock; (b) Houghton Mifflin Harcourt; **155** (tl) Rubberball/Superstock; (tr) Fransisco Cruz/Superstock; (bl) Ross Pictures/Botanica/Jupiterimages; (br) Chip Henderson/Index Stock Imagary/Jupiterimages; **156** (tr) © PhotoAlto/Getty Images; (cr) ©Getty Images; (b) © Dennis MacDonald/Alamy; **157** (bl) Sam Dudgeon; (br) Stockbyte/Getty Images; **170** (tl) Comstock/Jupiterimages; (t) Image Source/Superstock; (b) Lawrence Manning/Corbis; **171** (tl)

Illustration